LOOKING AFTER YOUR PET
Fish

Text by Clare Hibbert
Photography by Robert and Justine Pickett

Titles in the LOOKING AFTER YOUR PET series:

• Cat • Dog • Hamster • Rabbit
• Guinea Pig • Fish

First published in 2003 by Hodder Wayland
338 Euston Road, London NW1 3BH
Hodder Wayland is an imprint of Hodder
Children's Books.
This edition published under license from
Hodder Wayland. All rights reserved.

Produced by White-Thomson Publishing Ltd.
2/3 St. Andrew's Place, Lewes, BN7 1UP
Copyright © 2004 White-Thomson Publishing

Editor: Elaine Fuoco-Lang, Interior Design:
Leishman Design, Cover design: Hodder
Wayland, Photographs: Robert Pickett,
Proofreader: Alison Cooper

Published in the United States by
Smart Apple Media
1980 Lookout Drive, North Mankato,
Minnesota 56003

U.S. publication copyright © 2005
Smart Apple Media
International copyright reserved in all countries.
No part of this book may be reproduced in
any form without written permission from
the publisher.

Library of Congress Cataloging-in-Publication
Data

Hibbert, Clare, 1970–
Fish / by Clare Hibbert.
p. cm. — (Looking after your pet)
Summary: Explains how to take care of
aquarium fish, including setting up the tank,
choosing your fish, feeding them, taking care of
them when they are sick, and cleaning the tank.
ISBN 1-58340-435-X
1. Aquarium fishes—Juvenile literature. 2.
Aquariums—Juvenile literature. [1. Aquarium
fishes. 2. Fishes. 3. Aquariums. 4. Pets.] I. Title.

SF457.25.H53 2004
639.34—dc22   2003062390

9 8 7 6 5 4 3 2 1

Acknowledgments
With thanks to Fabrice Mascart of Vanishing
World, Herne Bay, Kent, and Aquatic Warehouse
Herne Bay, Kent.

The Web site addresses (URLs) included in this
book were valid at the time the book went to
press. However, because of the nature of the
Internet, it is possible that some addresses may
have changed, or sites may have changed or
closed down since publication.

Printed in China

Contents

Choosing fish

The first question to ask yourself is, "Why do I want fish?"

Fish are beautiful to watch and make wonderful pets, especially if you are allergic to fur or feathers. But before you decide to keep fish, be sure you are willing to look after them. Coldwater fish, such as goldfish, are not very expensive—but their tank can be. You must also find time to feed your fish every day and clean their tank every two weeks.

◀ A clean tank stocked with healthy fish a plants, is a beautiful thin to watch.

goldfish can live for eight years or more, but goldfish have been
own to live for more than 40 years (*see page 29*). You will be
ponsible for looking after it for all that time. Whenever you go on
cation, you will need to find someone to care for your pet.

▲ If you want to keep
tropical freshwater
fish, you will have to
heat the water in
the tank.

Pet Talk

What kind of fish would you like to keep?

• Coldwater fish include goldfish and shubunkins.
hese are the best pets for beginners.

• Tropical freshwater fish include tetras and guppies. They
eed warm water, so they are trickier to care for. See pages
4–27 for information about tropical freshwater fish.

▲ Shubunkins are happy in cold
water and have beautiful patterns and
coloring. This one has a fancy fantail.

Tank talk

Set up your tank before you get your fish.

You need to check the new equipment and let the water and plants settle so everything is ready for your new fish.

Tanks are sold in aquariums (specialty fish shops), pet shops, and garden centers—or look in your local paper for a cheaper, second-hand one. A tank 24 inches (60 cm) long, 12 inches (30 cm) wide, and 16 inches (40 cm) deep can house five or six coldwater fish.

▼ When choosing a tank, try to get the largest one possible

Checklist: fish kit

- Glass (or tough plastic) tank with lid and fitted fluorescent tube light

- Air pump

- Filter

- Pea gravel

- Plants

- Fish food

- Net

- Rocks or wood (but no sharp edges)

- Feeding ring (optional)

- Two thermometers: one to attach inside the tank and one to test water refills

- Cleaning kit including siphon (*see pages 18–19*)

o not be tempted by a pretty goldfish bowl. It is
oo small, and its narrow neck will not allow enough
xygen into the water.

e tank should have a lid (with a fitted
ht). This will stop your fish from jumping
t and keep dust off the water. You will
o need an electric air pump and filter to
ep the water clear.

Getting set up

Put the tank in its final place before you fill it with water.

First, clean the tank to get rid of any dust. Use plain, not soapy, water. Rinse the gravel and use it to line the bottom of the tank. Add some larger stones for your fish to hide behind.

Tap water contains a gas called "chlorine" that can kill fish. Leave tap water in a bucket for 24 hours so the chlorine escapes. If you prefer, buy dechlorinating tablets from the pet shop to make the water safe.

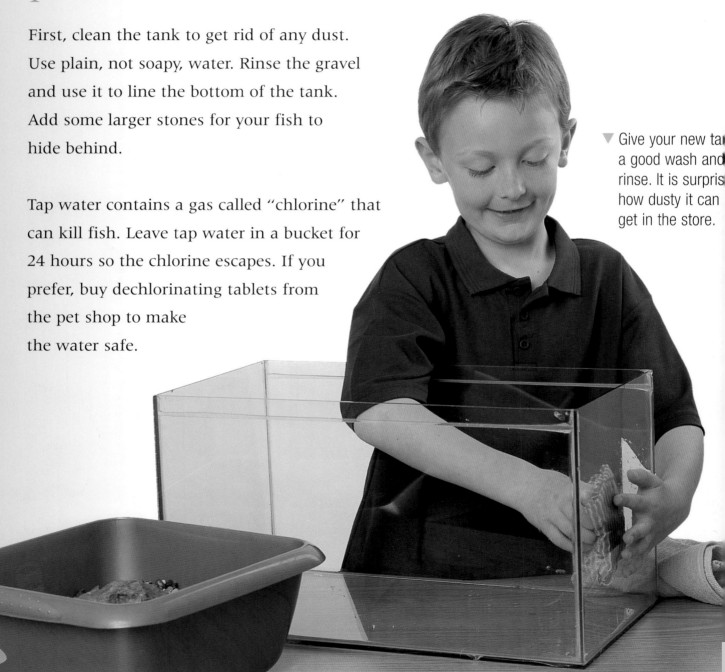

▼ Give your new ta a good wash and rinse. It is surpris how dusty it can get in the store.

Top Tips

Where to put your tank

 Put the tank on a steady surface—when it is full of water, it will be very heavy.

 Position the tank away from radiators or bright sunshine.

 Keep the tank out of reach of cats and other pets.

 Make sure you can reach the tank for feeding and cleaning.

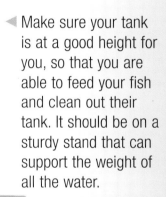

◄ Make sure your tank is at a good height for you, so that you are able to feed your fish and clean out their tank. It should be on a sturdy stand that can support the weight of all the water.

Plant life

Plants help to keep your tank healthy.

Plants help your fish by putting extra oxygen into the water. Oxygen is the gas animals breathe to stay alive.

Ask the staff in the pet shop how many plants you will need for your size of tank. Rinse the plants first, and put them into the tank when it is half-full. Some water plants come in plastic baskets, while others have bare roots. Bury the basket or roots under the gravel.

▶ To put in your plants, first scoop a dip in the gravel for the basket. Pile gravel around it to hold it steady in the water.

an adult to set up the
er and light and check
wiring. Then top off
tank with more
hlorinated water. Leave
tank for a couple of
rs. Check that the pump
d filter are working well.

u can put your plants
nywhere you like. They will
ake an underwater forest
r your pet fish.

Checklist: plant life

Here are some plants for coldwater tanks. Don't worry if you forget the
ames—you can always ask for advice in the shop.

- Arrowhead (*Sagittaria*)
- Cardinal flower (*Lobelia cardinalis*)
- Eel grass (*Vallisneria gigantean*)
- Java fern (*Microsorum*)
- Java moss (*Vesicularia dubyana*)

- Peace lily (*Spathyphyllum*)
- Pennywort (*Hydrocotyle*)
- Swordplant (*Aponogeton*)
- Waterweed (*Elodea densa*)

▲ Waterweed

▲ Cardinal flower

▲ Eel grass

Buying your fish

There are more types of coldwater fish than you might think!

Ordinary goldfish are handsome and hardy. They come in shades of red, orange, and yellow. There are also all sorts of fancy goldfish, including orandas, fantails, veiltails, and comets. You could try a dark, velvety moor or a colorful shubunkin.

Other coldwater fish that make good pets include weather loaches, bitterlings, danios, barbs, and ricefish. The aquarium staff will help you choose.

▼ Spend tim looking at fish before you choos any. Pick c ones that healthy an strong.

s best to put new fish
your tank in stages,
e or two at a time.
u should leave the
v fish in for about a
ek so they can settle
ore adding any more.

he aquarium staff will
ut your new pet in a
astic bag half-filled
ith water. Your fish will
e fine in the bag for a
hort time.

Top Tips

Choosing a healthy fish

Make sure you buy your fish from a pet shop or
aquarium that takes good care of its animals.

- The fish should be active, not lurking near the bottom.
- It should swim steadily, not tilt to one side.
- Its fins should be straight, not floppy.
- Its body should be well filled-out, but its belly should not be swollen.
- Its scales should be smooth and flat, with no white fluff or spots.

▲ Orandas are fancy goldfish that have a bulge on the
top of the head. This one is called a "red cap"
oranda—it is easy to see why.

Settling in

Never drop new fish straight into the tank.

The shock could kill your fish. Float the bag on the surface so that its water can reach the same temperature as the tank water. After about 20 minutes, unknot the bag and roll down the sides. When the water in the bag and the tank are at the same temperature, let a little tank water trickle into the bag.

◀ When you are carrying your new pet home, hold the bag carefully. Make sure there is enough water at the bottom for your fish.

entually you can pour out the bag.
ce the fish swim out, remove the bag
m the water.

ep the tank light off for the first day.
s will give the fish a chance to rest
er their journey. After this, turn the
ht on each morning and turn it off
h evening—to give your fish "day"
d "night."

se your thermometers to test the water
emperatures in the bag and the tank.

Top Tips

Your new fish

- Never touch your fish. You could damage their scales. Always use a net.
- Sudden temperature changes are very bad for fish.
- Ask at the shop if your fish have been quarantined (kept away from other fish) to check for disease. If not, keep them in a separate tank for two weeks.

Feeding your fish

Feed your fish at the same time each da[y]

You can buy goldfish food from pet shops. Never overfeed your fis[h]. Follow the instructions on the goldfish food tub and take away a[ny] uneaten food after 10 minutes. If food sinks to the bottom, it ma[kes] the water dirty. You could also use a feeding ring (*see page 30*), which will make clearing away any leftover food much easier.

▼ Your pets will soon learn when it's dinner-time. They will come to the surface when you feed them.

Pet Talk

Going on vacation?

You can buy special food tablets that slowly release food for your fish. These are fine, but it is better to ask a friend or neighbor to come and feed your fish. At the same time they may be able to spot and treat any signs of illness.

Goldfish can eat other food, too. Try tiny pieces of lettuce and spinach, or even a few oats. These foods help fish that are constipated.

Fish love live food. You can buy this in aquariums. The two main types are daphnia (water fleas) and tubifex worms (bloodworms).

▶ You can buy live food in bags from your local aquarium. Your pets will love chasing water creatures like these daphnia (water fleas).

17

Cleaning the tank

It is your job to keep your pets' home clean.

Droppings and uneaten food make the water dirty, but y
cannot change all the water at once. Replace about a fift
of the tank water every two weeks. Use a plastic tube to
siphon the water into a bucket.

▲ Using a siphon is not difficult, once you get the hang of it.
Ask an adult to show you how the first couple of times.

Move the siphon through the gravel so it can suck up all the waste settled at the bottom.

Next, net the fish and put them in the bucket of siphoned water. Scrape off any green on the sides of the tank and remove any dead plants. Put the fish back and then, a little at a time, top off the tank with clean, dechlorinated water.

◀ You can clean the tank with the fish in it, but it is much easier to move them into a bucket of siphoned water.

◀ Treat the new water to get rid of chlorine. Use a dechlorinating tablet or leave the water to stand in a bucket for 24 hours.

Top Tips

Cleaning the filter

When you clean the tank, check the filter, too. The filter helps to keep the tank clear by sucking waste from the water. Ask an adult to help you remove the foam or wool. Rinse it in water from the tank or, if it is very dirty, replace it.

Sickness and health

You can help prevent disease by keeping the tank clean.

You should also check on the health of your fish at least once a day. If your fish has white fluff on its body, it probably has a fungal disease. Another problem is "white spot," caused by a tiny pest living on your pet. Pet shops sell treatments for these diseases that you put in the water.

▲ This fish has white spot on its fins, hea and gills. Eventuall the disease will co its entire body.

If you can, move the sick fish into a separate recovery tank—the others might pick on it if it seems weak.

Although it is difficult to take a fish to the veterinarian, you can still ask for advice. He or she may even make a home visit.

f your fish become pregnant, you should set up a nursery tank so the other fish do not eat the babies.

Pet Talk

Small fry

Healthy, happy fish might have babies! Goldfish lay tiny eggs, which stick to the leaves of plants. The adults often eat the eggs or baby fish, which are called "fry." If you want the eggs to hatch, move them to a nursery tank (a small tank without any adult fish).

Pond fish

Some fish are happy to live outside.

If you are lucky enough to have a pond, why not keep fish in it? You can also build your own—ask an adult to help. Make it at least 24 inches (60 cm) deep, so that not all the water freezes in winter. Use a tough pond liner to contain the water.

▼ Put plants in your pond. Your fish can hide among the stems—and even nibble at them, too.

mmon goldfish, comets, and some
ubunkins can all live in outdoor
nds. So can koi. These are
utiful relatives of the
dfish. The large ones
be very expensive.
ieves have been known
steal koi, so they are
a good choice if your
nd is in the
nt yard!

With their beautiful markings,
is no wonder that koi are
uch popular pond pets. Koi can
row to 12 inches (30 cm) or
nore if they have enough space.

Sometimes birds may come and steal your
pond fish. If you have this problem, you may
need to cover your pond with a net.

Top Tips

Outdoor ponds

- A pond is a bad idea if you have younger brothers or sisters. They could fall in.
- Build the pond away from trees, or put a net over it to catch fallen leaves.
- Stock your pond with plants for your fish to eat and use as shelter.
- Cover your pond with a net if birds or cats are hunting your fish.

Totally tropical

Tropical fish come in all sorts of amazing colors and shapes.

However, they need more equipment than coldwater fish. In addition to tank, lid, light, filter, and pump, you will also need a heater and thermostat. The heater warms the water. Position this near the air pump. The thermostat controls the heater to keep the water temperature steady.

▼ Set the thermostat to keep the water in your tropical tank at 75°F (24°C). Check this on the thermometer on the outside of the tank.

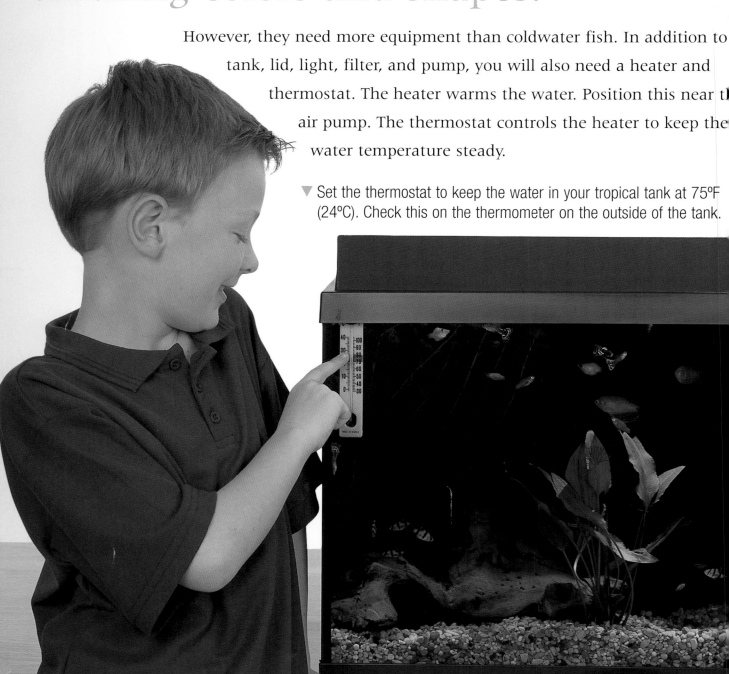

e best place to buy tropical fish is at

aquarium. Ask the aquarist to

lp you choose the right

uipment—and the right

h for your tank.

member to buy some

nts and tropical fish

od, too.

etras like to swim together
n schools. Neon tetras like
hese have a light-catching
tripe along their body.

Checklist: plant life

ere are a few of the plants that are suitable for tropical tanks. Your aquarist will be able to make some
uggestions, too.

- Amazon sword (*Echinodorus paniculatus*)
- Brazilian elodea (*Egeria densa*)
- Dwarf anubias (*Anubias barteri*)
- Dwarf crypt (*Cryptocoryne willisii*)

- Fanwort (*Cabomba aquatica*)
- Marble Queen (*Echinodorus cordifolius*)
- Pennywort (*Hydrocotyle leucocephalia*)
- Tropical sun (*Hygrophila rosanervis*)

▲ Amazon sword   ▲ Fanwort   ▲ Marble Queen   ▲ Tropical sun

Types of tropical fish

Choose fish that swim and feed at different depths.

You need hardy fish that will live happily together. Choose fish that like to live and feed at different levels of the tank; then the fish can all live together happily and have more room to swim around.

Surface feeders are fast-moving and have upturned mouths. They include the zebra danio, the glass catfish, and the Siamese fighting fish. Midwater fish stick to the middle of the tank. There are fast-moving tetras and barbs, as well as angelfish and gouramis.

▲ The Golden gourami is a peaceful fish, but it is best to keep two males in the tank together—one might bully the other.

...tom feeders usually have a down-turned ...uth and a flat underside. They suck food from ... tank's bottom and sides—and help keep it ...an! They include the clown loach, pleco, and ...ne catfish, such as the suckermouth.

... tank stocked with fish that feed ... different levels is called a ...ommunity tank.

Plecos stick to the bottom of the tank, vacuuming up any algae that is growing there. Choose carefully, though. Some plecos can grow to be 24 inches (60 cm) long—or more.

Pet Talk

Tropical types

There are two types of tropical fish: freshwater and marine. Marine fish are used to living in the sea. Because they need the right amount of salt in the water, as well as the right temperature, they are best left to the experts. When buying tropical fish, check that you are buying freshwater ones.

Fish facts

Bet you didn't know that Egyptian pharaohs kept coldwater fish in their palaces! Read on for more fantastic facts.

- Chinese emperors were keeping pet fish in ponds around 1,000 years ago. They took the hobby to Japan 500 years ago.

- Europeans began keeping pet fish in the late 1600s, after explorers came back from the East with tales of the beautiful ponds they had seen.

- Tropical fish come from a warm part of the world called "the tropics"—the area between two imaginary lines that circle Earth called the "Tropic of Cancer" and the "Tropic of Capricorn."

There are more than 100 different kinds goldfish.

Most pet fish are harmless, but some ople keep piranhas! Piranhas come from uth American rivers. A school of them strip an animal to the bone in minutes.

A pregnant goldfish is called a "twit."

The record for the longest-living goldfish is d by Goldie, which celebrated its 43rd thday in January 2003.

Goldfish fry are brownish-gray. It can take a r for them to turn orange. In their last years, dfish sometimes turn silvery.

Pond fish hibernate when the ather gets really cold. Their ies slow down and they not need to eat. y become active in in the summer, en temperatures rt to rise.

Glossary

Air pump
A machine that pumps bubbles of air into the tank. The movement of water helps to create more oxygen and gives the fish a current to swim against.

Algae
A kind of seaweed that grows in aquariums.

Allergic
Having a bad reaction (such as a skin rash or difficulty breathing) to something such as fur, feathers, dust, or a certain type of food.

Aquarist
Someone who works in a shop that sells pet fish.

Aquarium
(1) A fish tank. (2) A shop that sells pets that live in tanks, such as fish and turtles. (3) A fish zoo, where there are tanks of fish on display.

Chlorine
A type of gas that is put in tap water to kill germs. However, it can also kill fish, so use only dechlorinated water in your tank.

Coldwater fish
Fish that come from cooler waters, such as goldfish. Coldwater fish are used to water temperatures between 53 and 75ºF (12–24ºC).

Constipated
Not able to go to the bathroom properly.

Dechlorinating tablet
A tablet that can be added to water to remove the chlorine and make it safe for fish tanks.

Feeding ring
A plastic ring that floats on the surface of the tank. Sprinkle a pinch of fish food inside the ring to make it easier to clear away uneaten fish food.

Filter
A machine in the tank that takes in water, sieves out particles of waste, and then puts back the cleaned water.

Fluorescent
A type of light suitable for fish tanks because it does not heat up like an ordinary light bulb.

Freshwater fish
A fish that comes from rivers or lakes, rather than the sea.

Fry
Young fish.

Heater
A machine used to heat the water in a tropical fish tank.

Hibernate
Enter a sleep-like state. Pond fish often hibernate during the cold winter months.

Marine fish
A fish that comes from the sea, rather than rivers or lakes, so it is used to being in salty water.

Oxygen
A gas that all animals need to breathe. You take in oxygen from the air using your lungs. Fish take in oxygen from the water using their gills.

Quarantined
When an animal, such as a fish, is kept away from other animals in case they are carrying a disease.

Siphon
A plastic tube that can be used to suck up water from the tank.

Thermostat
A machine used to control a heater. It can keep the temperature in a tropical tank steady.

Tropical fish
Fish that are used to warmer waters, for example tetras. Most tropical fish are happy in water temperatures around 75 to 80ºF (24–27ºC).

Further information

Books

Barnes, Julia. *101 Facts About Goldfish*. Milwaukee: Gareth Stevens, 2002.

Blackaby, Susan. *Fish for You: Caring for Your Fish*. Minneapolis: Picture Window Books, 2003.

Hamilton, Lynn. *Caring for Your Fish*. Calgary: Weigl, 2003.

Harvey, Bev. *Fish*. Broomhall, Penn.: Chelsea House, 2002.

Heinrichs, Ann. *Fish*. Mankato, Minn.: Compass Point Books, 2003.

Jango-Cohen, Judith. *Freshwater Fishes*. New York: Benchmark Books, 2002.

Silverstein, Virginia. *Fabulous Fish*. Brookfield, Conn.: 21st Century Books, 2003.

Useful addresses

The Goldfish Society of America
http://www.geocities.com/ Tokyo/4468/gfsa.html

The American Society for the Prevention of Cruelty to Animals (ASPCA)
www.aspca.org

Humane Society of Canada
www.humanesociety.com

Humane Society of the United States
www.hsus.org

Index